D0241513

THE LORD OF THE RINGS

THE TWO TOWERS

CREATURES

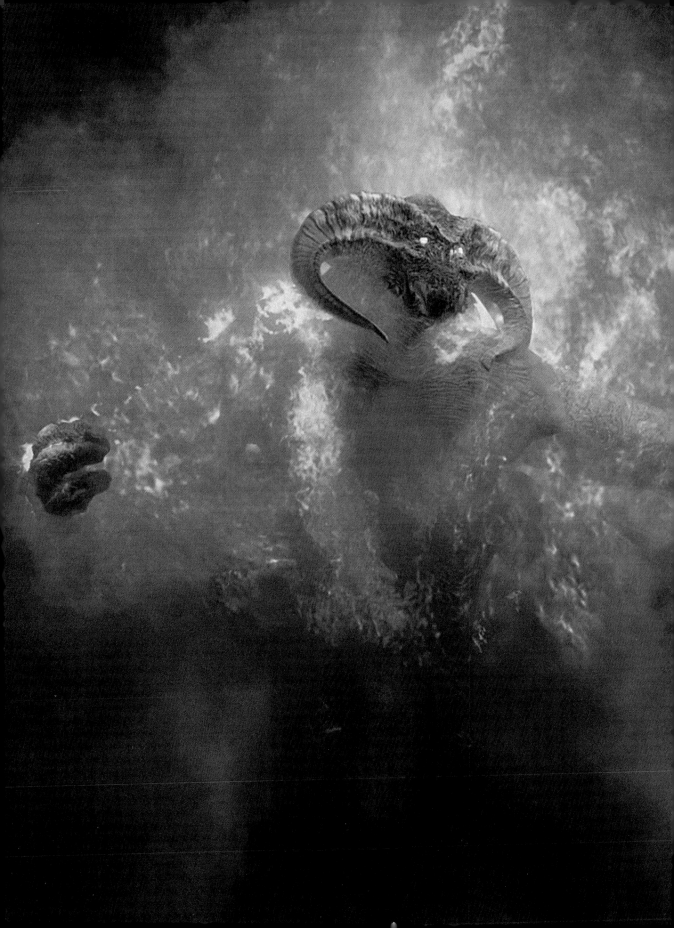

THE LORD OF THE RINGS

™

THE TWO TOWERS
CREATURES

Collins

An imprint of HarperCollins*Publishers*

First published in Great Britain by Collins in 2002

Collins is an imprint of HarperCollins*Publishers*,
77-85 Fulham Palace Road,
Hammersmith, London W6 8JB

www.tolkien.co.uk

9 8 7 6 5 4 3 2 1

Text by David Brawn; Design by James Stevens

Photographs, stills, artwork, film logos
© 2002 New Line Productions, Inc.
Painting of Tom Bombadil, detail from
The Willow-man is Tamed © Ted Nasmith 1995
Paintings of *The Dark Tower* and *Gandalf the Grey*
© John Howe 1989
Painting of *Oliphaunt* © Alan Lee 1991
Compilation © HarperCollins*Publishers* 2002
All Rights Reserved.

'The Lord of the Rings', 'The Fellowship of the Ring',
'The Two Towers', 'The Return of the King' and the
characters and the places therein, ™ The Saul Zaentz
Company d/b/a Tolkien Enterprises under licence to
New Line Productions, Inc. All Rights Reserved.

'Tolkien'® is a registered trademark of
The J.R.R. Tolkien Estate Limited.

The Lord of the Rings: Creatures is a companion to
the films *The Two Towers* and *The Fellowship of the Ring*
and it is not published with the approval of the
Estate of the late J.R.R. Tolkien.

The Lord of the Rings and its constituent volumes,
The Fellowship of the Ring, The Two Towers and
The Return of the King, are published by
HarperCollins*Publishers* under licence from
The Trustees of The J.R.R. Tolkien 1967 settlement.

A catalogue record for this book is available from
the British Library

ISBN 0 00 714409 1

Printed in Belgium by Proost

All Rights Reserved. No part of this publication may be
reproduced, stored in a retrieval system, or transmitted,
in any form or by any means, electronic, mechanical,
photocopying, recording or otherwise, without the
prior permission of the publishers.

To **SARAH** and **GEORGIA**, just two of a new
generation of Tolkien readers inspired by the films.

With thanks to the following designers,
who are quoted in this book:

Richard Taylor, Creature, Miniature, Armour, Weapons,
    Special Make-up Effects Supervisor
Paul Lasaine, Visual Effects Art Director
Christian Rivers, Visual Effects Art Director
Adam Valdez, Animation Supervisor
Dan Hennah, Set Decorator
John Howe, Conceptual Artist
Peter Owen, Make-up & Hair Designer
Peter King, Make-up & Hair Designer
Jim Rygiel, Visual Effects Supervisor
Randy Cook, 3D Sequence Lead Animator

and to the dozens of others who are not.

"*Culture is based in detail, in generations of characters, of people, of species, building on top of the past generation's work. In these films, there is not a buckle that isn't branded with the coat of arms of a particular army. Every rivet-head is detailed in some way. Every belt is hand-tooled to make it feel like it has been touched by the craftsmanship of the species that wears it. Hopefully, by doing this, the audience will gain a richer, more fulfilled perspective of the cultures that have gone on for thousands of years to generate the look of the period represented in the film.*"

RICHARD TAYLOR,
*Head of Special Effects and co-winner of two BAFTAs
and two Oscars® (Visual Effects and Make-up)
for The Fellowship of the Ring.*

"*I am sure that* The Two Towers *will be better than the first movie. This film is deeper and much more emotional.*"

BERNARD HILL, "King Théoden"

Introduction
CREATING CULTURES

The Lord of the Rings films are not monster movies. They do have their scary moments, of course, and the heroes encounter beasts and peoples who are definitely not of our world, but these are only supporting characters to the real stars of the films – the world of Middle-earth, and the story itself.

It is impossible to show here the extraordinary efforts and attention to detail the writers, artists, designers and film-makers went to over the last five years to turn J.R.R. Tolkien's celebrated books into realistic-looking films. However, this behind-the-scenes guide is intended to unveil a tiny piece of the magic in *The Lord of the Rings* movies.

"The most wonderful thing from our perspective was the development of the creatures. Although they are based in fantasy, we didn't at any time want them to feel so bizarre that the audience couldn't believe in them or accept them as players amongst the cast of Middle-earth. Therefore we tried to ground them as much as possible in the world that we know."

RICHARD TAYLOR

"The Elves, the Dwarves, the hobbits of Middle-earth all live in their own isolated communities. Just as in our world, where everybody's culture – European, American, South American, African, Australian – represents the evolution of those people through history, so it is in Middle-earth. This is why we have taken so much care in building cultural histories for the characters in these films."

PETER JACKSON, Director

HOBBITS

Hobbits are homely folk who live in holes in the ground in a little corner of Middle-earth called the Shire. As a rule, they keep themselves to themselves, enjoy the simple life, and like nothing better than good food (including two breakfasts!), tea, pipes and long naps. Sometimes known as halflings on account of their size, they can also be distinguished from other people of Middle-earth by their unkempt hair (though none have beards), their pointed ears, and their large, hairy feet.

"Hobbits are an earth-loving people, and there's something magical that should be celebrated about that. They are the essence of all that's beautiful and poetic about the human form, just as the Orcs represent all that is ugly and bestial about the human form. Hobbits have a kind of heroism, strength and size that's the opposite of their diminutive size."

SEAN ASTIN, "Sam"

"According to the book, Frodo is nearly 50 when he sets out on his quest, although it is still relatively young in the life-span of a hobbit. This is the first time I've played a 50-year-old!"

ELIJAH WOOD, "Frodo"

"They're only three feet six inches tall, but being short isn't an issue for hobbits. Which is cool, I think. In their world it's who you are from the inside that matters."

DOMINIC MONAGHAN, "Merry"

CREATURE FEATURE: HOBBIT FEET

"The feet took an hour and a half to put on every day. You slipped your foot in, and then they poured in glue, which was freezing cold, so you were stuck fast in this very, very tight shoe."

DOMINIC MONAGHAN, "Merry Brandybuck"

"The feet have a strange spongy, squishy feeling – I'd wear the same pair all day, except when I had to run around lots. Then I usually got through two pairs. If you stood on your toes they'd rip off!"

BILLY BOYD, "Pippin Took"

"When the weather got cold, your feet would go numb and the foam would absorb water – so you'd basically got ice cubes strapped to your feet."

SEAN ASTIN, "Samwise Gamgee"

"Those furry feet became the bane of our existence. They took so long to put on we lost an hour of sleep each night. On days our feet weren't due to be filmed, I'd say, 'We don't need feet today – we can stay in bed!' And they would reply, 'Well, there's a chance, so you must have them on.' Nine times out of ten I'd be right."

ELIJAH WOOD, "Frodo Baggins"

"I think Bilbo Baggins' feet must have been bigger than anybody else's. I was forever tripping over them and nearly falling flat on my face!"

IAN HOLM, "Bilbo Baggins"

Over the course of the film, 1,600 pairs of feet were made for the hobbits. Because they would damage easily on sharp rocks or stones, a "foot monitor" was on hand to provide emergency repairs. His name was Sean Foot!

The actors sometimes had to wear special boots on location so their hobbit feet did not get bogged down with mud.

THE "LOST"
TOM BOMBADIL

In the book *The Fellowship of the Ring*, the four hobbits encounter an ancient, red-faced man who lives in the Old Forest. Tolkien's readers have wondered why they did not see him in the film.

"We did contemplate having the hobbits walking through the forest, see a feathered cap come darting through the trees, hear the sound of Tom singing and have them turn and run away as fast as they could! We thought it would acknowledge Tom Bombadil in an affectionate kind of way for the fans, but we didn't have time to do it."

PETER JACKSON

"Maybe there's another film in which Tom Bombadil can appear in all his glory, but he's a big distraction in getting the story going. We haven't killed him off because he still exists in the novel – it's not as if we bought up every copy and destroyed them!"

IAN McKELLEN, "Gandalf"

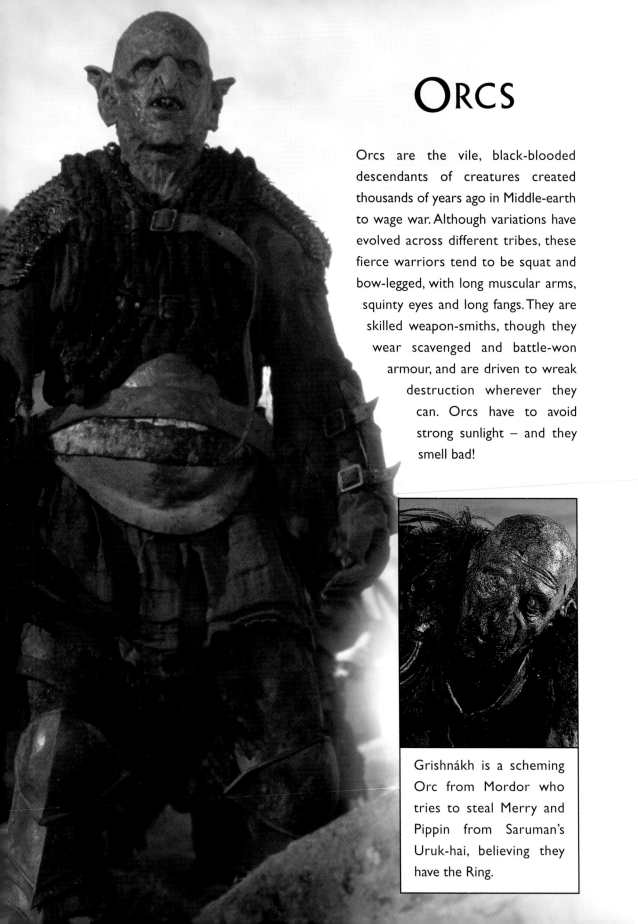

ORCS

Orcs are the vile, black-blooded descendants of creatures created thousands of years ago in Middle-earth to wage war. Although variations have evolved across different tribes, these fierce warriors tend to be squat and bow-legged, with long muscular arms, squinty eyes and long fangs. They are skilled weapon-smiths, though they wear scavenged and battle-won armour, and are driven to wreak destruction wherever they can. Orcs have to avoid strong sunlight – and they smell bad!

Grishnákh is a scheming Orc from Mordor who tries to steal Merry and Pippin from Saruman's Uruk-hai, believing they have the Ring.

WARGS

The Wargs of Rhovanion are giant wolf-beasts which have allied themselves to the Orcs. These "hounds of Sauron" are vicious and efficient hunters which patrol the plains of Rohan. Large enough to be ridden like horses, they can cover large distances without rest, and anyone who crosses the plains of Rohan does so at their own peril.

Sharku is an old and experienced Warg-rider who leads the charge against the Rohan refugees.

FROM THE DRAWING BOARD

Beginning with Tolkien's description of Wargs as evil wolves, the designers looked at other wild dogs such as hyenas, which were felt to have a more powerful and threatening appearance.

ELVES

The Elves are the wisest and fairest of all beings in Middle-earth. Tall and graceful, they love beautiful things, and their senses are keen and attuned to nature. Elves do not age or die, although they can be killed. Having flourished in earlier ages, the Elves' influence has waned as the dominion of Men has grown, and they are planning to leave Middle-earth for good.

FROM THE DRAWING BOARD

"Lothlórien was like the Swiss Family Robinson meets the Ewoks in a redwood grove. The look was misty, ethereal – Peter Jackson kept saying to keep it 'magical', like heaven."

PAUL LASAINE, *Art Director*

Galadriel is the oldest of all the Elves that remain in Middle-earth. Frodo tempts Galadriel to take the Ring, and for a few brief moments she is transformed by Sauron's evil spirit to look "beautiful and terrible as the Morning and the Night".

"Galadriel is a mixture of Mother Earth and physical glory, but there's also a sense of darkness and threat. I am a Ring-bearer myself as well as an Elf queen."

CATE BLANCHETT, *"Galadriel."*

"Three Rings for the Elven-kings under the sky"

Legolas is an expert with a bow and arrow, but the arrows he shoots in the films are all added digitally! By having the actor twang the empty bowstring, he could appear to shoot arrows better and quicker than possible in real life.

"To play Legolas, I had to learn archery, sword-fighting and horse-riding. I tried 20 different horses before I was given one to ride in the movies – and I still managed to fall off him and break a rib!"

ORLANDO BLOOM, "Legolas"

The Elf princess Arwen is faced with the consequences of falling in love with a mortal man. Her father wants her to go with the Elves rather than stay behind to grow old and die with Aragorn.

"The story of Aragorn and Arwen is an amazingly romantic love story. If I want to be with Aragorn, I have to give up my immortality. I have to choose between staying on Earth with my family and my people and being with him."

LIV TYLER, "Arwen"

CREATURE FEATURE: THEY HAD TEN THOUSAND MEN

"The motifs on the Elven armour were very nature-driven and spiritual looking, including leaf-shaped leather armour."

RICHARD TAYLOR

The great battle between the Elves and the Orcs at the beginning of the trilogy was filmed using real people plus thousands of computer-generated soldiers, created using a program called MASSIVE – Multiple Agent Simulation System in Virtual Environment.

Each digital soldier was made to look real by a program called GRUNT – Guaranteed Rendering of Unlimited Numbers of Things.

"We didn't know what these digital men were going to do. I still get a chuckle when I think about one of the first tests, where we had about 2,000 soldiers fighting, but in the background some of them were running away. I thought, 'Those are the smart guys!' It was extraordinarily spooky."

PETER JACKSON

GOLLUM

Gollum, or Sméagol as he was once known, is a ghoulish hobbit-sized creature who has been following Frodo. Centuries ago he found the Ring and, having killed his cousin Déagol, was banished from his home to live in a cave under the Misty Mountains, where he became twisted by evil and the solitude of living deep underground. When Bilbo Baggins came and took the Ring, Gollum found he could not live without it – he wants it back!

"Though Gollum has a strong presence in the book, his role in the movie will be huge. You can imagine a hobbit as a small person, and you can imagine what Gandalf will look like. But the creature of Gollum is going to be a revelation."

PHILIPPA BOYENS, Co-writer

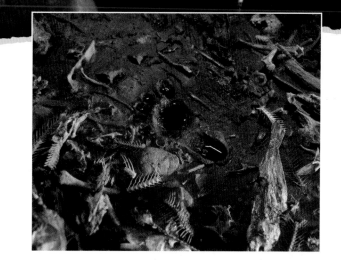

Gollum is created entirely using Computer Generated Imagery (CGI). The animators have worked to give Gollum realistic bone and muscle, all seen rippling under his translucent skin.

"I think that Gollum may be one of the most sophisticated digital creations seen yet. Throw out all your old ideas about what CGI looks like, because Gollum defies them."

RICHARD TAYLOR

Gollum's voice is provided by Andy Serkis, who also acted out all Gollum's scenes so the animators could copy a real person's movements. For this he had to wear a skin-tight suit with padded knees.

"Even though Gollum will be created by technology, Peter Jackson was determined that the part would be actor-led; something which is symptomatic of a production in which effects never take precedence over story, character or performance."

ANDY SERKIS, "Gollum"

THE ISTARI
SARUMAN

The Istari are the "wizards" of Middle-earth. Sent to help the mortal peoples in their fight against Sauron, they are forbidden from using their powers to confront evil, and must therefore rely on their wisdom and cunning.

The most senior of the Istari is Saruman the White, but his abuse of his powers and his allegiance with the Dark Lord lead him into conflict with his kinsman.

The only other Istari in *The Lord of the Rings* is Radagast the Brown, who unwittingly causes Gandalf to be captured. He does not appear in the films.

THE ISTARI
GANDALF

Gandalf the Grey's wisdom allows him to resist the temptation to take the Ring from Frodo, and he later sacrifices himself to save his friends. But he is transformed and sent back as Gandalf the White, more powerful and with an urgent mission.

FROM THE DRAWING BOARD

Gandalf the Grey was based on John Howe's famous painting, which was stolen at an exhibition in France and never returned. John has never painted Gandalf the White.

"Peter Jackson originally wanted Gandalf to have a three-foot long beard, but however good an actor Sir Ian McKellen is, we didn't think he could act through a three-foot beard!"

PETER OWEN, *Make-up & Hair Designer*

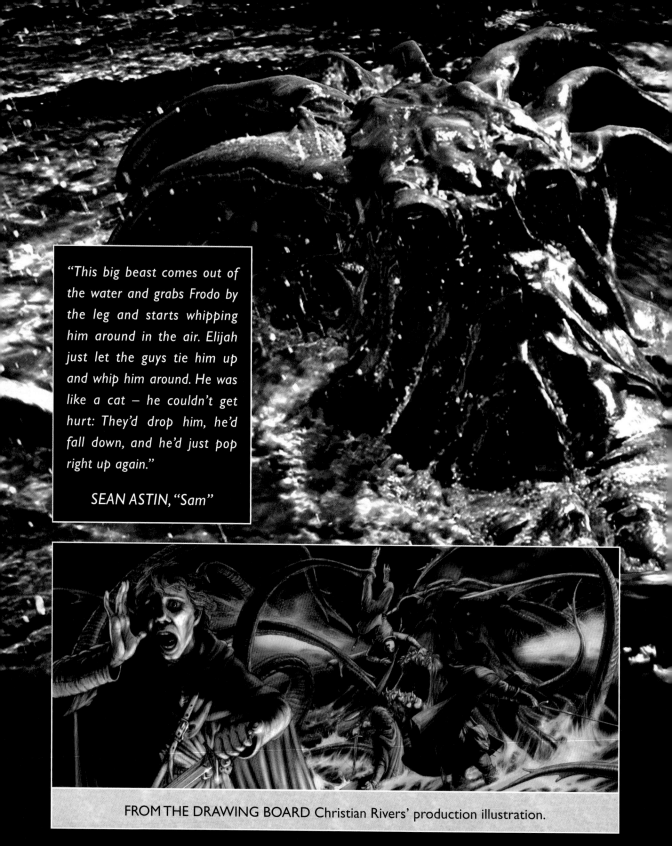

"This big beast comes out of the water and grabs Frodo by the leg and starts whipping him around in the air. Elijah just let the guys tie him up and whip him around. He was like a cat – he couldn't get hurt: They'd drop him, he'd fall down, and he'd just pop right up again."

SEAN ASTIN, "Sam"

FROM THE DRAWING BOARD Christian Rivers' production illustration.

"We put a lot of time into developing its eyes, to give it a look of an old man's intelligence, with puffy, soft, weepy eye sacs."

RICHARD TAYLOR

THE WATCHER IN THE WATER

When the companions are forced to continue their journey through the Mines of Moria, they are attacked at its entrance by the Watcher, a giant, squid-like creature that is disturbed when Merry starts skimming stones across its lake.

In his description of the fight with the Watcher Tolkien wrote, "twenty other arms came rippling out." However, the film-makers gave it just 12 tentacles, feeling that more than that would look messy and out of control.

The tentacles were designed so they ended in two "fingers" and a "thumb", with octopus-like suckers on the inside.

ENTS

The tree-like Ents are the oldest living inhabitants of Middle-earth. Looking like a fourteen-foot cross between a tree and a man, their skin is wrinkled like tree bark, with fingers like twigs and toes like roots. They are slow but strong, and are guardians of the forests. The leader of the Ents in Fangorn Forest is Treebeard.

"The Ents are angered by the Orcs chopping down trees around Isengard, throwing them into the furnaces which are smelting the iron ore to make weapons and armour for Saruman's army."

RICHARD TAYLOR

The Ents are realized as a combination of digital animation and full-size models. They have been the trickiest of all the creatures in the films to get right, not only on account of all their leaves, but mainly because trees which walk and talk are traditionally only seen in comedy!

The voice of Treebeard is provided by John Rhys-Davies, who also plays Gimli.

"At least I didn't have to physically play the role," he says. "That would have been too much!"

DWARVES

Dwarves are a noble race, fiercely proud of their own culture and code of honour. Great miners and craftsmen of the mountain-halls, Dwarves are also courageous warriors, although they are quick to anger and do not trust other races.

"A Dwarf is short and stout, so we decided that Dwarf armour should be square and boxy and geometric."

RICHARD TAYLOR

The correct plural of the word *dwarf* is *dwarfs*, but J.R.R. Tolkien chose instead to use the "incorrect" dwarves, because it went better with *elves*. After writing *The Hobbit*, he said that he wished he had used the real "historical" plural for dwarf, *dwarrows* – a word he finally used in *The Lord of the Rings* when naming their great city.

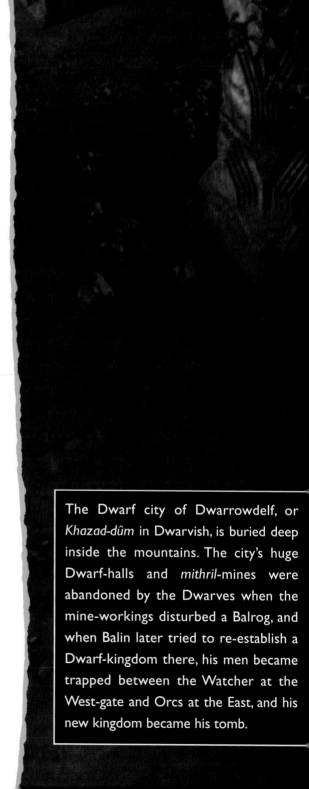

The Dwarf city of Dwarrowdelf, or *Khazad-dûm* in Dwarvish, is buried deep inside the mountains. The city's huge Dwarf-halls and *mithril*-mines were abandoned by the Dwarves when the mine-workings disturbed a Balrog, and when Balin later tried to re-establish a Dwarf-kingdom there, his men became trapped between the Watcher at the West-gate and Orcs at the East, and his new kingdom became his tomb.

"Gimli is a wonderful character! Suspicious, paranoid, quick to quarrel, yet he shows unquestioned loyalty to Aragorn, and his protectiveness towards the little hobbits is endearing. Above all, there is his fearlessness in the face of overwhelming odds, so that even when confronted with certain death, he will always turn and fight!"

JOHN RHYS-DAVIES, "Gimli"

GOBLINS

"Goblins" is a name used by peoples of Middle-earth to describe Orcs, and is particularly applicable to the Moria Orcs. They have evolved differently from those which live above ground, remaining short and developing larger eyes to enable them to see in the dark. They wear spiky, jagged armour to help grip the rock when climbing the subterranean structures.

"The issue was making it feel as if the Orcs had built their armour and weapons. We were fortunate that we could always go back to the bible, the written word of Tolkien, who went to incredible lengths to describe this world."

RICHARD TAYLOR

Because the extras needed to be small, many of the Orcs ended up being played by women and girls.

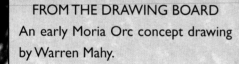

FROM THE DRAWING BOARD
An early Moria Orc concept drawing by Warren Mahy.

For some of the Moria Orcs, the make-up was augmented with digital eye enlargements to give them the crazed, open-eyed look Peter Jackson wanted.

TROLLS

Trolls come in various shapes but generally only one size – large! Bilbo knew them to be powerful yet dim-witted creatures when the three he encountered in *The Hobbit* were turned to stone. But they can be a real menace in battle, as Frodo and his companions find during their skirmish with a cave troll in Balin's tomb.

"The cave troll has the physical nature of a huge sumo wrestler. He's a huge blundering idiot of a creature until his temper gets up and he just can't help himself. Even his friends, the goblins, are bashed aside if his swing gets too manic."

RICHARD TAYLOR

To make it clear that the troll is the orcs' slave, designer Randy Cook added a leash around its neck. By making it a chain, the troll then had an additional weapon to use in the fight.

The encounter with the cave troll occupies less than half a page in Tolkien's novel, yet is expanded into 3 minutes 45 seconds of screen time in the film.

"On set, the Orcs were there but the cave troll wasn't. For filming, there was a foam cut-out of it, with markers for its eyes, nose and mouth. It was more of a reference for the cameras than for us, but it gave us an idea of its size."

ELIJAH WOOD, "Frodo"

CREATURE FEATURE: CREATING THE
CAVE TROLL

Though the Fellowship have to kill the ten-foot cave troll, or else it's going to kill them, the film-makers did not want it to feel like a victory. That the seriousness of their quest has driven them to kill an unwilling combatant is not something any of them should feel good about.

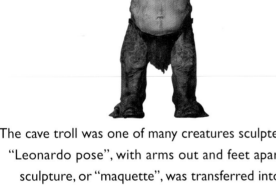

The cave troll was one of many creatures sculpted in the "Leonardo pose", with arms out and feet apart. The sculpture, or "maquette", was transferred into the computer as a 3-D digital model using a device originally invented to scan carcasses for the New Zealand Meat Board!

"I really didn't want the creatures to look like computery monsters. In creating the cave troll, for example, we gave him fingernails that are dirty and broken, and a skin that is covered in burns and warts."

PETER JACKSON

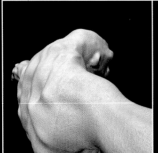
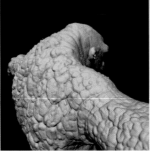

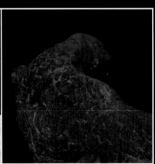

FROM THE DRAWING BOARD These images show how detailed skin texture was added on the computer.

CREBAIN

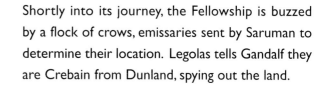

Shortly into its journey, the Fellowship is buzzed by a flock of crows, emissaries sent by Saruman to determine their location. Legolas tells Gandalf they are Crebain from Dunland, spying out the land.

"Ian McKellen had to look at these birds, which he had to say were spies. He used to call them spies from Star Wars!"

ELIJAH WOOD, *"Frodo"*

Rather than go out and film real crows, the Crebain were all animated by computer. Each bird was created separately from a library of information about how birds fly, and each one was programmed with a bird "brain" to stop it crashing into other birds. Finally, the computer animators had to direct the flight of the flock — real birds would never have flown in the right direction!

The moth does not feature in Tolkien's books, although Bilbo's poem "Errantry" does refer to imaginary insects known as Dumbledors!

MOTH

Imprisoned by Saruman at the top of the Orthanc tower, Gandalf summons a messenger in the form of a moth to get help.

The moth used in the film was a Gum Emperor Moth. *"For reasons of animal welfare, the scene had to be shot to coincide with the moth's life-cycle. So we kept the larva in a cupboard with a hot-water tank until we were able to film that stunning close-up of the insect in Gandalf's cupped hands and release the insect ito the wild."*

DAN HENNAH

"He was sort of a Supermoth, able to fly a thousand miles per hour and reach the top of this huge tower. We had to walk a line between complete reality and dramatic performance!"

ADAM VALDEZ

GWAIHIR

LORD OF THE EAGLES

Gandalf is finally rescued from the wrath of Saruman by his old friend Gwaihir. The giant eagle saved Gandalf 60 years ago during the events in *The Hobbit*, when the wizard and his journeymen were attacked by Goblins during their quest to burgle Smaug the dragon's treasure. Gwaihir's loyalty to Gandalf means that he surely has not seen the last of him...

FROM THE DRAWING BOARD
An early colour test by Paul Lasaine

Gwaihir is seen only fleetingly in *The Fellowship of the Ring*, as both he and the Gandalf figure astride his back are computer-generated animations.

RINGWRAITHS

Nine rings were gifted to the race of Men, who
above all else desired power. But the promise
of eternal life did not turn out the way they
expected: the nine mortal men now exist in a
state that is between life and death, ghoulish
spirits under Sauron's control. When Gollum
finally reveals the location of the One Ring,
they are sent out on their black, flame-eyed
horses to find "Baggins" in the Shire.

Only Frodo has ever seen the true form of the Witch King and the other Ringwraiths. The
terrifying skeletal cadavers of undead flesh, although they walk like people and need beasts su

"Nine for Mortal Men doomed to die"

FELL BEAST

Having lost his horses at the Ford of Bruinen, the Witch King later takes to the skies on a massive Fell Beast, a winged dragon-like creature.

"Watching the first Fell Beast taking shape in the computers was amazing! I was thinking, 'This is great! I'll never again have to draw things like this from scratch!' I'll just phone Weta Digital and say, 'One Fell Beast, please, three-quarters back-view, from above, wings up!'"

JOHN HOWE, *Conceptual Artist*

FROM THE DRAWING BOARD
John Howe's version of a Fell Beast, painted for a book cover in 1989.

EASTERLINGS

The Easterlings are first spotted by Frodo and Sam at the Black Gates of Mordor. A primitive, militaristic people from Rhûn in the east, these long-standing adversaries of the people of Gondor have been recruited by Sauron to join in all-out war.

The last element of the Easterlings' exotic armour to be finalized was the helmet. It was decided to give them visors because hiding the face makes the warriors beneath look less human so it is less controversial to show them being killed in the film.

WILD MEN

The primitive Woses live in the Druadan Forest and are commonly known to the Rohirrim as the Wild Men. Their bitter resentment is stirred up by Saruman, who incites them to take up arms and accompany his Orcs in a rampage of destruction through the Rohan villages.

"One day, Peter Jackson announced that we were about to film 50 Wild Men and we just didn't have the wigs. We had to cobble together 50 wigs from the old 'dogs', half-bald wigs left over from other films, and we used five different colours of mud, hand cream and Vaseline to make them look disgusting."

PETER KING

> "The Balrog took the longest time to realize. Tolkien's description was hard to translate – a shadow blacker than black, with a mane of fire on a creature that was vaguely a shape. A man shape? We didn't know."
>
> CHRISTIAN RIVERS

> "Since the Balrog was moving around and running, real fire would have blown out or wafted about in a weird way. We had to animate it in a way that it would not be too real."
>
> JIM RYGIEL

> "Its skeleton was a mixture of a dog and a bull, with the horns of a ram, the tail of a lizard and wings of a bat. The skin was made to look like lava when it cools and cracks."
>
> RICHARD TAYLOR

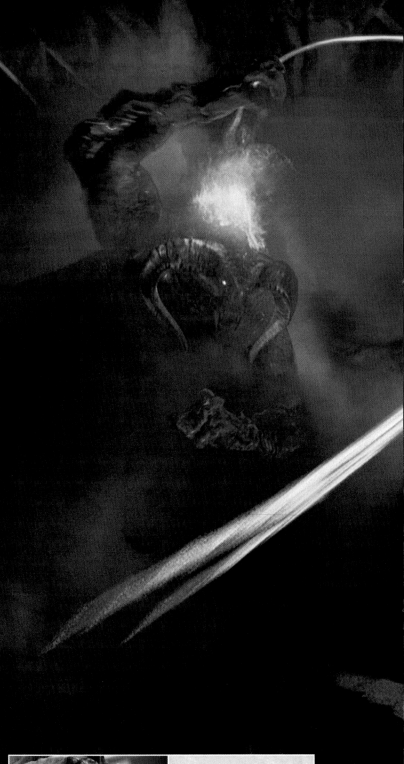

FROM THE DRAWING BOARD
Ben Wootten sculpted a four-foot model of the Balrog's head.

THE BALROG

The Balrog is the last of a race of ancient fire-demons which has slumbered beneath Moria for thousands of years until disturbed by the Dwarves, mining for the precious *mithril*. Huge, winged, shrouded in fire and wielding a whip of flame, the Balrog is a fearsome nemesis – even the Orcs fear it.

Dragging Gandalf off the bridge of Khazad-dûm to the depths of the mines, the Balrog's flame is temporarily extinguished by the fall. But Gandalf's ordeal is not over, and when the beast is rekindled, he must continue his fight to the death…

For the Khazad-dûm sequence, a fourteenth-scale model of the great hall, staircase and bridge was constructed – a massive set 21 feet tall, 66 feet long and 45 feet wide that took four months to build. From the moment the Fellowship see the Balrog coming, to where Frodo is carried out at the end, all the sets are models – the longest continuous miniature sequence ever for a film.

MEN

By the time of the Third Age, during which *The Lord of the Rings* takes place, the men of Middle-earth have divided into many peoples. The noblest, whose forebears formed an alliance with the Elves against Sauron, are the Gondorians. The kingdom of Gondor, whose capital is the White City of Minas Tirith, has come under constant attack from other groups, including the Easterlings and Haradrim.

Allies to Gondor are the Rohirrim from the north, whose reputation as "Horse-lords" is built upon their affinity with horses. They rule a territory called the Riddermark, and their chief settlement is the wooden city of Edoras.

Aragorn is a Ranger, a wandering northerner, who has chosen a nomadic lifestyle despite his birthright as a true prince of Gondor. He has yet to realize that Sauron fears him above anyone else.

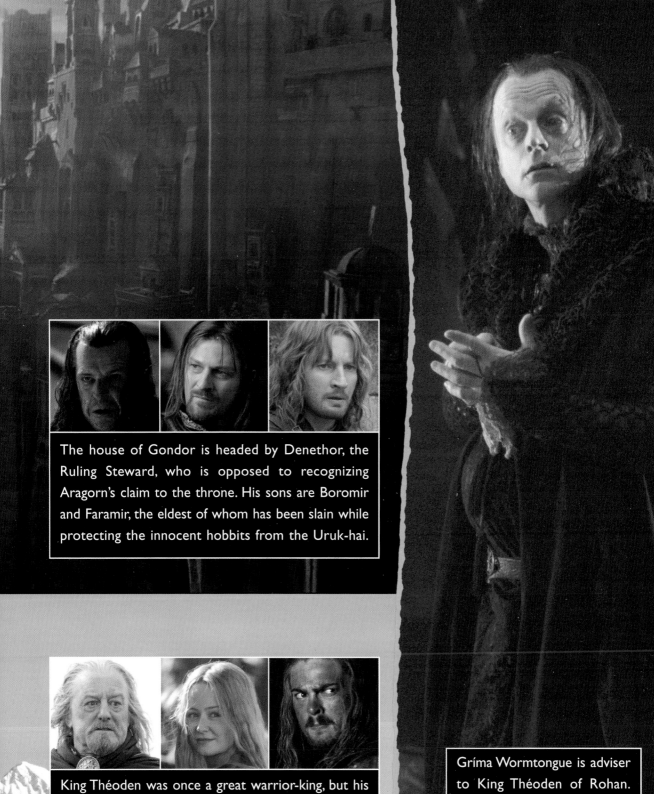

The house of Gondor is headed by Denethor, the Ruling Steward, who is opposed to recognizing Aragorn's claim to the throne. His sons are Boromir and Faramir, the eldest of whom has been slain while protecting the innocent hobbits from the Uruk-hai.

King Théoden was once a great warrior-king, but his spirit has been broken. His son, Théodred, is killed by Orcs, and his niece Éowyn and nephew Éomer, both orphans, are struggling to determine their roles in the destiny of Rohan.

Gríma Wormtongue is adviser to King Théoden of Rohan. He is not to be trusted, because his true master is the wizard Saruman, who wants to conquer Rohan.

THE URUK-HAI

The Uruk-hai are Orc and Goblin hybrids bred by Saruman to use as soldiers. Unlike other Orcs, they are tall, strong, and are unaffected by sunlight. When his influence over King Théoden is broken by Gandalf, Saruman sends his army of ten thousand Uruk-hai warriors to wipe out the last bastion of Rohan soldiers at Helm's deep.

Beserkers are the largest and most terrifying of Saruman's Uruk-hai. They wear no armour and are marked in war-paint with the sign of his White Hand.

Tolkien named his creatures after the Old English word *orc* meaning "demon". He invented the word *uruk* as a Black Speech alternative, so this Mordor name imitates the unnatural evolution of Orcs into Uruks.

"The Uruk-hai was possibly one of the most enjoyable pieces of creature design for us. Tolkien never really went into how Saruman bred them, so Peter developed this alchemy to bring the Uruk-hai from the earth. Creating the prosthetic characters to be born like soggy potatoes dug up from the caverns by the Orc gaolers was an amazing period in the making of the films."

RICHARD TAYLOR

CREATURE FEATURE:

LURTZ

Saruman sends his Uruk champion, Lurtz, to capture the hobbits with the Ring, but Lurtz is killed in close combat with Aragorn.

The most elaborate make-up in the films was for the birth of Lurtz. Beginning at midnight, actor Lawrence Makoare was encased in a body suit and then smothered in sticky goo. The make-up was finished just in time for filming to begin at ten o'clock the following morning.

MÛMAKIL

The barbarian Haradrim are feared for their use in battle of the giant tusked Mûmakil (the hobbits call them Oliphaunts). Equipped with huge war towers on their backs to carry archers and spearmen, these 50-foot elephant beasts are impervious to arrows and strong enough to crush everything in their path.

HARADRIM

The Haradrim are swarthy invaders from Harad, far to the south-east. These exotic outlanders wear bright clothing and ornaments, but they are seen as servants of tyranny for their attacks on the southern borders of Gondor.

The Haradrim costumes were inspired by the twelfth-century Saracen warriors of the Middle-east. Early designs suggested they might wear less clothing and more jewellery than they do in the films.

SAURON

Sauron is the Lord of the Rings. Thousands of years ago he established a stronghold in Mordor and built the dark fortress of Barad-dûr. Seducing the Elves, he oversaw the forging of the Rings of Power, but kept the One Ring for himself, before losing it in the great battle at Mount Doom. Now seen only as a great Lidless Eye atop his tower, he is working tirelessly though dark agents to get the Ring back so he can complete his conquest of Middle-earth.

Sauron's armour consisted of almost 200 separate pieces, and was made in both steel and plastic for different shots.

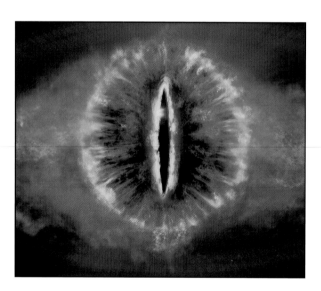

"No one could get a grasp of what the Eye of Sauron actually was. Even Peter Jackson spoke of it in very vague terms – 'it needs to be kind of fiery'. After trying several different looks, we came up with a cat's eye, which is the creepiest-looking eye of all. The Eye of Sauron had the smallest role in the film, but it took the longest to conceive."

JIM RYGIEL, Visual Effects Supervisor

Sauron uses the Palantíri, legendary seeing stones made by the Elves, to spy on things far away. It is through a Palantír that Sauron has been gaining control over Saruman.

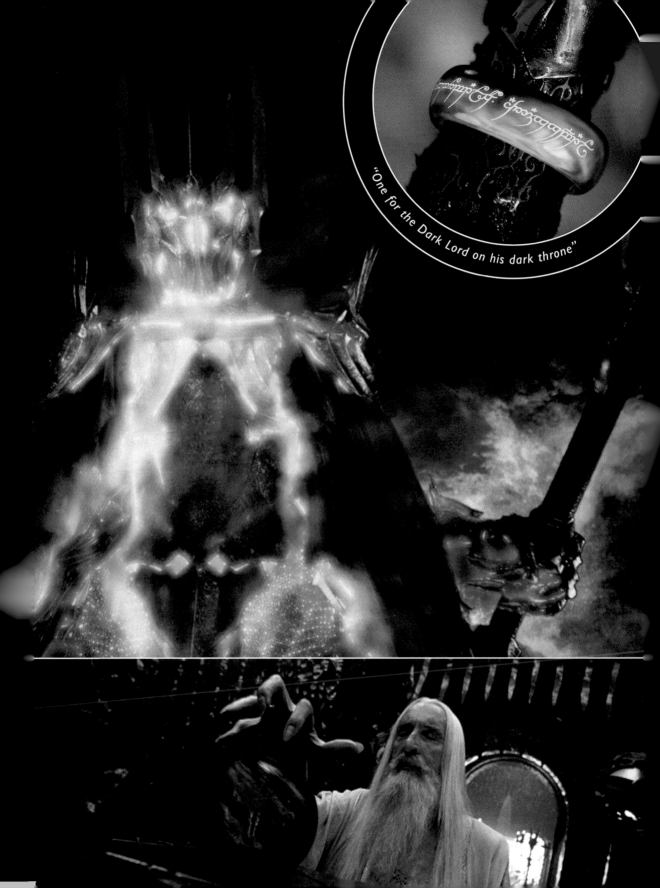

"One for the Dark Lord on his dark throne"

SHELOB

When Frodo and Sam find their rou[te]
to Mordor through the Black Gate[s]
blocked, Gollum suggests another w[ay].
But Gollum is not to be trusted.

For his suggested route will take the[m]
through Cirith Ungol, the foul lair [of]
the evil Shelob…

To be concluded in…

THE LORD OF THE RINGS
THE RETURN OF THE KING